When We Were Little

When We Were Little

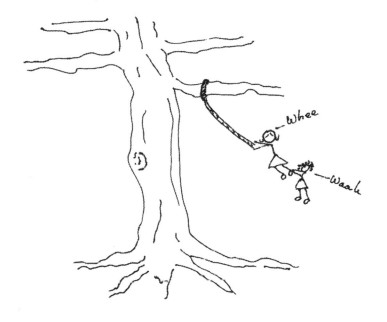

LOIS LOWER

WHEN WE WERE LITTLE

iUniverse books may be ordered through booksellers or by contacting:

iUniverse
1663 Liberty Drive
Bloomington, IN 47403
www.iuniverse.com
1-800-Authors (1-800-288-4677)

ISBN: 978-1-4917-8167-8 (sc)
ISBN: 978-1-4917-8168-5 (e)

Library of Congress Control Number: 2015918039

Print information available on the last page.

iUniverse rev. date: 12/01/2015

Memories by
Lois Lower

With complicity by
Joyce Lloyd and James C. Bush, Jr.

Dedicated
To Poor Nancy

Who was born after we were Big

"I had a farm in Africa," wrote Danish author Isak Dinesen, "at the foot of the Ngong Hills".

Well, when we were little we had a farm in Idaho, at the foot of the Holbrook hills.  It was one thousand acres of 'dry farm', raising wheat and alfalfa hay, a few pigs and chickens and cows, and children.

There were two of us to start with: Lois, the eldest, and Joyce, eighteen months younger. We were born in the Great Depression, but when we were little that meant nothing to us. All we knew was food to eat, clothes to wear and a bed to sleep in. And a grand and glorious outdoors to play in.

Our outdoors was all dirt in the early days, that's the way it is with farms, and when we were little sometimes we wore shoes in that dirt and sometimes we did not.

The 'highway' in front of the house went down to Holbrook. It was graveled, but there was another little road that cut off at an angle to go down to the neighbor's that was lovely soft dirt, just right to walk barefoot in. The main thing about the dirt road was the big black 'stink bugs' that lived on it. They were some kind of black beetle, an inch or more in length, stalwart fellows sturdy enough to make you pause before trying to pick one up. If you stepped on one, or if one got run over, its distinctive odor would linger for hours. So we never stepped on one on purpose, but what we did do was stop and tickle them with an outstretched barefoot toe. The touching would make them stop too, and raise their rear end in the air in defensive mode, preparatory to letting loose their stink. How we would laugh to see them stuck there in the middle of the road, rear ends aloft, waiting for the next attack that never came.

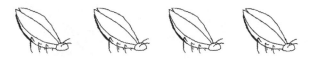

The house was old and its once white paint was now weary with the years. There was a welcoming porch across part of the front, a step up from the ground, with three lovely carved posts along it, just right to grab with your hands and swing around on. The highway out front was

 up on a slight hill and the house sat on the edge of that rise. The farm yard dropped away from the house down to a little creek and then swooped up again so that the furthest fields were climbing to the mountain behind.

The house yard was surrounded by a delightful picket fence. There was a solid board laid flat on top of the fence posts, and the pickets were nailed to the outside of the flat board, thus providing a surface for the adventurous to walk. When we were little we were very adventurous!

The slope directly behind the house led down past a dirt root cellar and a two-hole outhouse to the chicken coops at the bottom of the hill. Two-hole outhouses are fancier than one-hole outhouses, but when we were little the most exciting thing that happened there was the day the little bum lamb walked in, jumped up on the seat and fell through a hole! Lambs can be adventurous also, but our Daddy and the hired man didn't think that was a good thing. It took a long time to get the lamb out and we had to go to the house so we couldn't listen.

On the side of the chicken coops there was another board fence that could be walked on but we were not quite adventurous enough to walk it very often. That fence was made of large wide boards nailed vertically side by side and the flat walking board was over our heads. There was a nice  tree next to the fence that could be climbed to get to the walking board, but it needed a  great deal of effort.

There were many interesting buildings on our farm, and when we were little we played in all of them. Most were lined up in a row with the chicken coops, thus running along the bottom of the slope. There was a garage with a scary grease pit in the middle of it. There were long boards over the pit, no doubt to keep the children out of it, but when we were really little we never dared to peek under for fear the monsters who lived there would jump out. After we had grown some, some real monsters came to live there, but that is the story of the skunks and I'll tell it in a minute.

Next to the garage was a shed with a nice sloping roof. It sheltered a collection of odd pieces of machinery which,

if our Daddy was safely out
in the field, could be climbed
on to gain that roof and gaze
regally out at the surrounding
farmyard. Next to the shed
was a log building we called
the granary. It housed grain,

of course, sometimes loose and sometimes in bags, but the
neatest thing in the granary was the big grinding wheel.
It had a seat on it like a bicycle, and pedals attached to the
wheel in the front, only the wheel was a big round
whetstone and was mounted high off the ground. Daddy
would sit on the seat and push on the pedals and sharpen
an edge on his tools, or maybe on the cutter bar of the
mowing machine. It was both scary and thrilling to watch
him hold an axe blade to the turning wheel and see the
sparks fly. He said the sparks wouldn't hurt, but we didn't
dare get too close.

Next came the long pole gate that led out into the
fields. At the other end of the gate was the pigpen where
the great big scary momma pig lived. (When we were little
there were a lot of scary things.) Sometimes she had babies
and we would stand on a rock and look over to watch
them. Our Daddy liked that old momma pig, he said she
had big litters and took good care of them. Our Mama
said she was the gentlest pig she ever saw. I suppose we ate
some of the babies and sold some of them but we didn't
worry about that. What else is there to do with pigs?

The pigpen was the corner of the barnyard, for the big two-story barn was attached to the side of it, and the barn pointed back up the hill toward the house. The barn had been built to keep hay on the second floor and had a huge window on the side with a beam going out to hold the hay fork. In our time the hay was kept in the 'stack yard' behind the barn, and we were not supposed to play on the second floor but it was such a lovely great open space to run in and play games that sometimes we couldn't resist.

We played all over. We played in the barn, we played in the granary, we played in the chicken coops and got dirt in our hair for there was dirt on the roofs, and possibly scared the chickens out of laying the next day's eggs. One of our favorite places was the cubby hole on the side of the old combine that was kept in the stack yard behind the barn. Oh, what a lovely playhouse that was. Big enough for both of us to get in at once, but small enough to be cozy, and, best of all, not easily seen from the house. Sometimes it was a cave, sometimes a tree house for Tarzan and Jane who lived there often, sometimes a castle for princesses to hide from wicked witches, and sometimes Flash Gordon planned excursions against the evil Martians who always said "Aaarrgh" when their plans were thwarted.

How did we know Tarzan and Jane, Flash Gordon and the Martians who said "Aaarrgh"? Well, on Saturdays when we went to the big town to buy groceries our Grandma took a newspaper with the Saturday 'funny papers'. And then on Sunday mornings we listened to Uncle Roscoe (or somebody) read the Sunday funnies on the radio. What a great invention radio was! What a great invention 'funny papers' were!

We'll have to eat in the kitchen again...

Going to town on Saturday had its drawbacks. When we were little we had many toys to build things with. We had Tinker Toys and Lincoln Logs and modeling clay. And we had clever little things called Krazy Ikes, little plastic bodies with little knobs to attach heads and arms and legs in the proper places. The pieces were different colors so you could get many different effects. One particular time we had a marvelous landscape laid out on the dining room table, houses with the Lincoln Logs and fences with the Tinker Toys, a little blue pond with the clay, and a wonderful windmill with the Tinker Toys, complete with a wheel to turn on the top. We made people and animals with the Krazy Ikes and the clay, and had a good time playing for several days, making the big folk eat at the kitchen table. Then we went to town.

When we came home that night, the next door neighbor, who was often our hired man, had been in the house and hung one of the toy farmers from the windmill! He never denied it, and it was weeks before we forgave him. It was also several weeks before we could go to town without worrying about our toys.

Years later, when we were very, very big, we met a nephew of that hired man who told us that the hired man used to tell his nephews "Lois and Joyce stories" and admitted hanging our farmer. We were offended. The very idea!

We had pets to play with too. Cats came in all kinds of colors and sizes, but they were all barn cats. When we were little cats were not allowed in the house, but

nevertheless one of our Mama's best stories had to do with a cat and a rattlesnake.

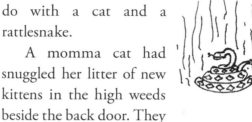

A momma cat had snuggled her litter of new kittens in the high weeds beside the back door. They

were very small, and unbeknownst to momma cat, that morning there was a hungry rattlesnake also in the weeds, looking for breakfast!! When our Mama came out the back door, she and the cat saw the snake at the same time. Momma cat went on the attack!

Our Mama said that was the wildest battle she had ever seen, as the cat would dart in, trying to get the snake by the neck, and dart back out before the snake could strike her. Our Mama was also concerned about having a rattlesnake loose in the house yard where her children played. When the snake began to ease away from the kittens, our Mama ran for the shovel and chopped him in two ugly pieces!

"Thank you" said momma cat.

"You are indeed welcome" said our Mama.

We had dogs. All farms need dogs. Somebody has to bark at the cows and the strangers at the gate. The first dogs on the farm were Billy and Jack. We really don't remember them, but we saw their pictures in our Mama's photo album, and she told us stories about them. We were babies when we moved to the farm, and our Mama could let us play outside without fear for Billy never left us alone. Mama could always see Billy's tail when she couldn't see us.

And we would mourn when she told us about Jack. He was a black dog with a long sturdy tail that would sometimes knock us over when we were too little to defend ourselves. One day our Daddy got tired of picking us up after Jack knocked us over and he cut Jack's tail off with the ax. Ooh, we would cry when she told us. Poor Jack. But our Mama said Jack didn't carry a grudge.

The next dog we had was named Pecho. Our family went to Las Vegas to visit our Mama's family, and our Uncle Bob sent Pecho home to live with us. We thought he was special because he had a Spanish name. He was a skinny brindle-colored dog, with a long tail. Our Daddy didn't have to cut his tail off because by then we weren't babies any more and he couldn't knock us over. Farm dogs don't have fences because it is miles to the next farm, so Pecho could run where he pleased. One day he didn't come home. And the next day he didn't come home either. Many days later our family was out riding around in the hills and we found the remains of a dead dog. Our Daddy said it was Pecho because he was wearing Pecho's collar. Our Daddy said he must have found somebody's poisoned coyote bait and ate it. We were sad to think he died alone in the hills.

Lots of people had dogs and cats, but we had one pet nobody else had. Our Mama raised a baby magpie. Its name was Maggie, of course. It was very little when our Daddy brought it home. It couldn't eat big bird stuff, so our Mama would mix up boiled egg yolk and milk in a bowl and feed it with a little baby spoon. When Maggie got bigger she would eat out of the bowl herself, and when she got very big our Mama would cut her little scraps of meat, because, said Mama, magpies were scavenger birds and would eat the flesh of dead animals in the hills. Sometimes we could help feed her, but sometimes she would get impatient and bite our fingers if we were too slow.

Our Mama spent a lot of time talking to Maggie and petting her. She was not allowed to go outside until she got very, very big because Mama was afraid she would learn to fly and fly away. Maggie did learn to fly but she did not fly away, she stayed by our house. She also learned to talk! She would say her own name, "Maggie, Maggie" and she would say Joyce's name too, and when Mama would scold her she would say "Okaaay," but I don't remember what else she could say. I do remember one time when the family was driving to Grandma's house we put Maggie in a bird cage and took her to town with us to prove to our Uncle George that she could, too, talk! Our Grandpa had a lovely head of thick white hair that we liked to comb. One time he came to visit on the farm and as he was sitting in his rocker on the porch Maggie came to perch on his shoulder and combed his hair with her beak.

When we were little our job in the evenings was to pick up a basketful of chips from the wood pile to be used for kindling the next morning to cook breakfast. When Maggie came to live with us she liked to help, but she would throw the chips out of the basket as we would throw them in. And when we would scold her she would scold right back.

But Maggie's story had an unhappy ending. One spring day some men from Holbrook had been out hunting and stopped by our place to visit with our Daddy on their way home. One man was holding his gun as he stood outside the car. They mentioned that they had shot a few jack rabbits and magpies.

"Well, don't shoot any magpies around here" said Daddy, and as he said it Maggie flew up to the house from the barnyard. Without thinking, the man swung up his gun and shot. Our Daddy used some of the words he used when the lamb fell in the outhouse and told the man he had better leave fast. Our Mama screamed (using words we didn't know she knew) and ran to pick up her pet. She sat in the rocking chair for a long time, crying and petting our poor dead Maggie. Daddy got supper that night.

The ladies in Holbrook were all mad at the man. "Oh" said his wife. "Everybody in town but you knew that Lucile had a pet magpie!"

When we were little winters on the farm were fun for us. Playing in the snow was fun. We had our own sledding hill, from the house down to the barn. We could build snowmen and throw snowballs. One time when there was snow on the road our Daddy took us to school in Holbrook in the buggy driving old Sam. Did we have sleigh runners instead of wheels? I don't remember. But another time I do remember riding to school on old Sam behind my Daddy. Sam had long legs and could easy walk through the snow.

We did go to school sometimes when we lived on the farm but it wasn't near as much fun as playing in the barnyard.

One time all the folks in town decided to have a sleigh-riding party. In the winter many farmers put sleigh runners on their hay wagons so they could drive out in the fields to feed their cows. The bed of the wagon had high sides on it and there was clean hay in the bottom of it. The horses pulled the sleigh along the roads picking up neighbors. There were lots of grown-ups and little kids and everyone was standing on the sides watching the scenery go past, but one side must have had more people than the other for suddenly the wagon bed tipped over and all the people fell in the snow. Nobody was hurt but it was scary. We had to wait till all the men put the wagon bed back on the runners and we could drive on. We must have gone somewhere to have refreshments. I don't remember that part, but that was what you did after a sleigh-riding party.

The wind blew a lot in Holbrook. The winter we were almost big the wind blew snowdrifts as tall as we were in the front yard. As the snow settled and got kind of hard we decided to dig a snow cave in one big drift. After school and on weekends we would get shovels and dig away. After a while we could sit in our cave, but we kept digging because we wanted to stand up in it. But a sad thing, by the time we could stand up in it, it got to be spring and the snow began to melt. The roof fell in!

We didn't stay sad very long, because spring was fun too, when we lived on the farm. We could hardly wait for the ground to dry out and the weather to get warm enough to go outside without our heavy winter coats. When we were little we loved to play outside just as it was beginning to get dark, running in circles and laughing. Our Mama would tell us to put our coats on, but we would take them off and throw them on the porch when she wasn't looking.

There was a high bank on the road just a little way from our house. The dirt was kind of like clay and you could dig holes in it. One time we were playing by that dirt bank on a spring afternoon. The weather was so warm and the spring air smelled so good that before we knew it we had taken off our shoes and stockings and were walking around in that dirt barefooted. We waved at the neighbor lady from way up the road as she drove by. Very soon our Mama came walking up the road with her switch. The neighbor lady had stopped and squealed on us! For shame, going barefoot in the cold weather. But we didn't catch our death of cold, either.

We listened to the radio a lot when we were little. Our Daddy liked to listen to the news programs, and our Mama liked to hear the stories in the afternoon, all about ladies having adventures. I remember "Stella Dallas," and "Our Gal Sunday," and an old grandma lady named Ma Perkins. We liked the stories that came on later, after we got home from school, about kids having adventures. Especially we liked "Jack Armstrong, the All-American Boy" and we wanted to eat Wheaties like Jack did, but we got to eat mush instead, oatmeal and corn meal and cracked wheat. But Cream of Wheat was more fun, because we got to listen to "Let's Pretend" on Saturday mornings. We used to sing the Cream of Wheat song, and I can still remember it

"Cream of Wheat is so good to eat
And we have it every day
It makes us strong as we go along
And it makes us shout Hooray!

It's good for growing children
And grown-ups too to eat
For all the family's breakfast
You can't beat Cream of Wheat!"

(applause please)

One thing I remember about the radio when we were little was the night the Martians came. We were having neighbors stay for supper. It was dark. Our Daddy and the men were down at the barn doing the evening chores, the ladies were helping our Mama fix some supper, and the radio was on. Nobody was paying attention when suddenly the announcer announced that Martians had landed in New Jersey and the authorities had called out the Army and Navy and who knows what all to fight back! These guys didn't even say Aaaargh. They just started killing people. Mama and the ladies were frightened.

"We've got to get the men so they can listen," they said. Mama was a fraidy-cat so one of the other ladies went out in the dark and got the men from the barn. By the time the men came running up the hill the announcer was talking again. Some guy named Orson Welles was presenting a program called "The War of the Worlds" because it was Halloween! Well, when we were little Halloween was no big deal, and we didn't know any guy named Orson Welles, and we were all scared silly! After a while we could laugh, but we remembered that night for a long time. When we got big we learned that people all over the country had been scared silly, too.

Another thing about the radio was December 7, 1941. Our Daddy was listening to the news program instead of going to church that morning and heard the announcer talk about the Japanese planes bombing Pearl Harbor. We didn't know what Pearl Harbor was or who the Japanese were, but it was all the radio people could talk about for a long time.

When we were nine and seven years old, our Mama came home from the hospital with a baby brother. His name was Jimmy. Our Daddy used to call him Jiminy Cricket, after the cricket in the movie "Pinocchio." We were offended. Nobody called us Snow White or Cinderella.

We thought he was a live doll just for us to play with. When he could walk around and talk a little we called him Janie and made him play house with us. And made him wear dresses. He didn't always like it, but he was too little to fight back. Sometimes we would play house in the old granary, but sometimes we would just play in the middle of the barnyard. We would borrow our Mama's broom and sweep the dirt into long lines to make the walls of our house.

The last dog we had on the farm was a big long-haired collie kind of dog named Shep. He was mostly black with white on his belly and around his face. He was a grown dog when he came to live with us and we liked him a lot.

One day we discovered that he liked Jimmy the best. We were all out in the front yard one day when a strange man drove up and came in the yard. Our Daddy and baby Jimmy started to walk toward the man when Shep began to growl and got between the man and Jimmy. Daddy asked our Mama to take the baby because he was afraid Shep might bite. We moved to town when we were almost big and Jimmy was two years old. Shep followed Jimmy everywhere and protected him for many years. The whole family was sad years later when Shep protected almost-big Jimmy from a porcupine. It took our Daddy hours to pull the quills out with the pliers and poor Shep died not too many months later.

Jimmy was with us one time when we had an exciting adventure up in the mountains with our Daddy and our Uncle George. Daddy and Uncle George wanted to go shoot rabbits and magpies. They let us go along, but they left us in the car. Jimmy was in the front seat and we were in the back, with the other gun. We began to play with the gun and accidentally touched the trigger. Boy, did that make a loud noise! Boy, did Daddy and Uncle George run fast to get back to the car! There was a hole in the roof of the car, but we didn't even get spanked.

There were a lot of rabbits around our farm, but there were a lot of skunks too. Our Daddy hated skunks. We thought they were pretty, all fat and round and black and white, but they were scary. If you got too close they would turn around, lift their tail and spray you with a terrible smell. It was much worse than the stink bugs. One time when we were little our Uncle Lester came to visit on the farm. When Uncle Lester came he and our Daddy would laugh a lot and play tricks.

This time they decided it was time to get rid of the skunks. Oh, they plotted and planned but nothing worked. Every time they killed a skunk, the skunk would spray as it died and get its revenge. They shot one, they beat one with a stick, they tried a bonfire, they tried to catch one in a cage and drag it. They tried every mean thing they could think of, but nothing worked. They still got sprayed and had to take a bath. Our Mama and our Aunt Blanche would laugh and laugh.

Finally they decided to starve one to death, thinking it wouldn't spray if it died of starvation. It took them days to lure a mama skunk into the garage so they could push her into the pit in the middle of the floor. And then she had babies! We don't know what the mama skunk ate, maybe mice, but she lived a long time. Our Daddy put boards over the hole so we wouldn't fall in, but we would push the boards aside and lay on our stomachs to watch the skunks. The babies were cute. The mama skunk didn't seem to mind us looking at her. Uncle Lester finally had to go home and never did know whether our Daddy got sprayed. And we don't remember what happened to mama skunk either.

We didn't see many coyotes around the farm, but one time we were riding in the back seat of the car when our Daddy was driving the neighbors home after they had been helping him. The road went past the wheat stubble field and they saw a coyote walking along. "Let's get him," said Daddy, and drove out into the field to chase the coyote with the car. The men all yelled and hollered and the coyote ran fast. I bet he didn't come back to that field again.

There were different kinds of animals on the farm. Besides dogs and cats, and pigs and chickens, we had cows and horses. The cows were not much fun. Our Daddy would milk them in the morning and then put them in the pasture. At night he would bring them back into the barnyard to be milked again and stay the night. Sometimes we would go with our Daddy and help him walk behind the cows. We could watch him milk. That was kind of fun.

But the really fun part was watching the milk be poured into the big separator in the house. The milk would run down through little metal circles and the cream would be separated from the milk. Our Daddy liked to put cream on his cereal and our Mama would make butter out of the rest of it.

Horses were different. The grown-ups got to ride them, but we were too little. Our Daddy rode a big horse named Sam. He was brown and had long legs. Our Uncle Ronald called him "old High and Mighty." "He goes up mighty high and comes down mighty hard," Uncle Ronald would say. At first there were driving horses to pull the hay wagons, but then our Daddy got a big tractor to pull the wagons and we only had Sam and the derrick horse left. The derrick horse would pull the cable on the big fork which would lift the hay from the wagon to the top of the stack.

We wanted to ride the derrick horse but our Daddy said we were too little. Beth got to do that. She was a neighbor who had her own horse and was almost big enough to be grown up. She got to do lots of things we couldn't do, but we liked her anyhow. One time our Daddy borrowed a Shetland pony to see if we could ride him, but he wasn't friendly and we didn't like him so Daddy sent him home.

Just before we were big there was a horse called Lady. She was a pretty red color but when her colt was born he was black all over. When he was brand new his legs were all funny and knobby, so that was what we named him – Knobby! He was not afraid of anything and would walk right up to us and snuff our hair. When he got to be bigger than we were, we were afraid of him and would holler when he snuffed our hair. One day when we hollered our Daddy got mad and hit Knobby with his fist on the side of his head. Knobby's head was hard and Daddy hurt his hand.

One of the things about summer was that we got to play in the garden. The garden was down the hill on the side of the house, on a different side from the outhouse and the chicken coop. Our Daddy would plow it up and mark out very straight rows with his great big ball of string. He was very fussy. Then we would help our Mama plant the seeds. They called it helping, but it was more play to us. We loved to drop the big yellow corns and the little green circles of peas and think about what they would look like growing up. Every day we would go down the hill and see if something had come up in the night. It took a long time. The carrots would come up first and we would wait impatiently for them to get big enough to eat. We would pull the little baby carrots, rub the dirt off on our skirts and eat them right there in the garden. When the peas grew up we liked to eat them standing in the garden too.

"Don't play in the garden," our Daddy would say. "You're going to step on something". When it was haying time or time to harvest the wheat our Mama would cook a big meal at noon for the hired men and we would get to go to the garden and bring up whatever was big enough to eat. We would help to snap the beans and husk the corn but that wasn't as much fun as eating baby carrots.

One summer when we were almost big we had a bad plague of grasshoppers. Our Daddy had planted grass in the front yard by then so we didn't have to walk in the dirt. The grasshoppers were all over the grass and the gravel walks and in our Mama's flower beds. We had to wear long pants all summer and so did Mama. Sometimes we even wore rubber bands around our ankles to keep the bad grasshoppers from crawling up inside our pant legs. They didn't bite us, but they were scary. Our Grandma in town didn't have grasshoppers at her house. I guess it was too far for them to walk.

At the end of the summer all the farm ladies would do what they called 'canning', which always made us laugh because they put the food in bottles, not cans! We liked it when our Mama would can peaches. We could eat them while we helped, but our favorite thing was when it was time to can tomatoes. We would have some tomatoes in a pan and we would sit on the picket fence in the front yard, with a tomato in one hand and a salt shaker in the other and eat till we were full. And sometimes we would have tomato juice running down our dresses. That is the best way to eat tomatoes.

Christmas was fun on the farm. Our Daddy would drive up in the hills and bring home a cedar tree. Sometimes we got to go with him. We always got to decorate the tree. The best place to put it was in the corner where the radio was. We would make chains out of colored paper and hang on lots of shiny icicles made out of something you could see through. We always would go to the Christmas play that the big kids at school put on. One year I got to be the only little kid in the big kids' play. The big boys teased me to see if I had my part memorized yet. Yes, I said, and to prove I was as smart as they were I recited my part. I can still remember it.

"Me too, Me too, Hello, Me too"

We would go to bed early on Christmas Eve so we could get up early! We got paper dolls and coloring books and books. Always we had books. Nearly every year we each got a new doll. One year our Mama made cloth dolls that were big enough to sit in a chair. One had blond yarn hair and the other had brown. Their names were Snow White and Rose Red, like in the fairy tale. And that year our Daddy made painted beds for the dolls, big enough they could lay down in them.

We would have breakfast and then after our Daddy had done the chores we would drive to town to Grandma's. Not only did we get more presents, like more paper dolls and coloring books, but we would have cousins to play with. We liked cousins, even if they were all boys. Our Grandma would fix dinner and then while the grown-ups talked we would color in our books or we might read from our books to the littler cousins.

We would see our cousins in the summer too. All the family came to our Grandma's house for Memorial Day. After dinner every one would go up to the cemetery and visit relatives, like our Daddy's brother who died when he was young and other Grandmas and Grandpas that we never got to know. Then again all the family came to Grandma's for the 4th of July. The big parade always came past Grandma's house, and then we went up to the Square for the kid's races and came back for dinner. Dinner at Grandma's house was a big thing to do.

Sometimes our Mama was adventurous also. One summer our Daddy found a great big water tank that he attached to the windmill. It was tall, as tall as the windmill, and so wide that even the biggest hired man couldn't reach across it. One day our Mama and the neighbor lady that lived down the road decided they wanted to swim in the tank. They put on their swimming suits and let us put on our swimming suits too. We climbed the ladder up the windmill and then very carefully walked across the wide board to get into the tank. Mama and the neighbor lady went first and then reached out their hands to help us in. The water was nice but it was a little scary because we couldn't let go of the side of the tank. It would be a long way to the bottom. I think our Daddy didn't think it was a very good adventure because we never did it again.

There were not a lot of cars that used the highway in front of our house. There were a few more farms up the road from us and then it was just dirt for a long way to another highway. One evening an old car pulled up and the man asked our Daddy if they could camp by the wood pile for the night. They built a little fire and had some supper. We wanted to watch them but Daddy said that wouldn't be good manners and we had to come in the house and watch out the window instead. We wondered where they were going, on a road that didn't go anywhere, and if they were pioneers who had a car instead of a covered wagon. We wondered if they were just being adventurous too. In the morning, their car was gone.

The summer we were almost big we moved to town and left the farm behind. Lois was eleven and Joyce was nine. It was a new world for us, an elegant house to live in, many friends who lived close by and a school bus to ride every morning. We each got to bring our favorite cat, and we were enchanted to learn that we were going to raise rabbits, lots of rabbits, who were as soft and cuddly to play with as our cats. Jimmy brought Shep, who immediately began a years' long fighting rivalry with Tex, our Uncle Marion's dog. Tex lived with our Grandma and he thought we children belonged to him too. Our Daddy brought his black horse Knobby who just got bigger and bigger, and eventually went to live with a big man that needed a big horse to ride. I guess our Mama brought her pleasure, after ten years of living on the farm, at having the city blessings of electric lights and an indoor bathroom!!

We grew bigger and bigger ourselves, all of us, and went out into the world and had many adventures but we were never again as free and light-hearted as when we were little and lived on that farm at the foot of the Holbrook hills.

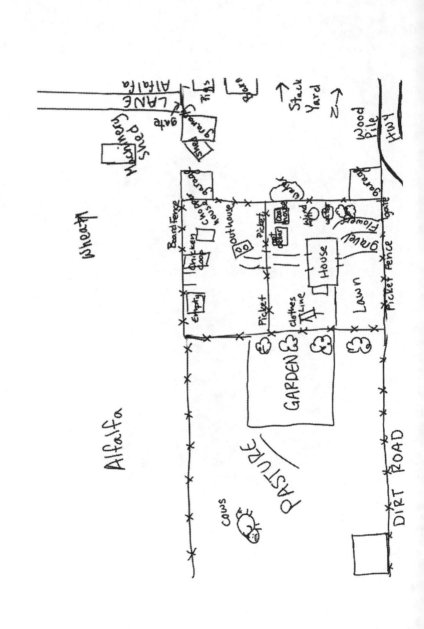

The Holbrook Farm
Pictures Taken June 1981

The Holbrook House
It Faced East

The windmill was next to the house on the north.
Stock watering tank right over the
fence on north side of windmill

The coal house was right behind the big house.

The farmstead was down the slope to the west. The
granary on the left, two-story barn on the right,
with the pigpen (now torn down) in between.

Cousins at the Window of the Barn Loft
Tom Lower on Top
Andy Lower on Bottom
Bushes and Lloyds in Between

Three curious horned owls check out visitors.

Wearing "Bush Hats"
Siblings Rest in Door of Granary
Jim Bush on Top
Joyce Lloyd on Left
Lois Lower on Right

Small Log Building We Used
For a Play House Located
By the Chicken Coop

Printed in the United States
By Bookmasters